The Operator's Code

Leadership Lessons from War Rooms, Boardrooms, and Everything in Between

Built, Not Written

Ashok Madhav Tamhankar

Dedication

To my parents;for the roots that grounded me, the resilience that carried me, and the quiet strength that taught me what it truly means to lead without applause.

Epigraph

"Not all leaders stand at the front.Some hold the line in silence, steadying the chaos, stitching the gaps, and making progress possible."

Table of Contents

Preface

This book wasn't planned. It didn't emerge from a sabbatical or a spark of inspiration. It came together in the margins of real work, between overflowing calendars, unplanned escalations, and those late-night pauses when everything else had finally gone quiet.

It came from a place I know well: the middle of the mess. Where decisions are made without perfect information. Where systems are held together by intent, not instruction. Where leadership doesn't happen in all-hands meetings, it happens quietly, in follow-ups, rewrites, and second chances.

Over time, I realized something: There are enough leadership books that show you how things *should* work. There aren't enough that show you how it actually feels.

This isn't a collection of frameworks. It's a set of field notes. Written for those who lead in pressure zones, whose performance isn't always seen, but whose presence is always felt.

If you've had to explain a missed deadline without blaming your team... If you've led a call while silently taking the hit for something you couldn't control... If you've held your ground while letting others take the credit... Then you're exactly the kind of leader this book is written for.

This isn't about theory. It's about decisions. Clarity. Quiet conviction. And staying steady when everything around you isn't.

It's not comprehensive. It's not clean. It's honest.

And it's yours.

This may not be the whole playbook. But for now, it's the part that matters.

Welcome to The Operator's Code.

Ashok Madhav Tamhankar

Acknowledgments

This book may carry my name on the cover, but its pages bear the fingerprints of many.

To the teams I've had the privilege to lead, thank you for trusting me, challenging me, and staying in the arena when it would have been easier to step back. You didn't just execute the plans; you helped shape the path.

To every colleague who gave me space to grow, even when I didn't have it all figured out, your grace mattered more than you know.

To the mentors who showed me that leadership isn't about perfection, but about persistence, this book is stitched with the quiet lessons you never even knew you were teaching.

To those who stood by me when I questioned my own voice, you reminded me why it was worth finding again.

And to Shaheen, my constant, my critic, my calm. Thank you for being the mirror I needed, even when the reflection was uncomfortable. This book, like so much else in my life, carries your quiet influence in every line.

Chapter 0: The Operator's Lens

"Leadership begins with perspective. And sometimes, the clearest view comes from behind the lens."

You've been here before. Called at 7:45 a.m. to explain something that broke at 2:00 a.m. Stayed late to rework a plan that changed because someone forgot to update the brief. Picked up the phone when no one else wanted to. Calmed a client, covered for a colleague, escalated without creating panic. You've shipped things no one thought would get done, and kept the lights on when systems, or people, failed.

And you did it all while keeping the team steady, the narrative clean, and the machine moving forward.

If any of that feels familiar, this book is for you.

The lens doesn't just reflect, it frames. So does leadership. It shapes how we see, what we notice, and what we choose to respond to. This book is about that lens. About how operators see the work, and what it takes to keep moving even when the picture isn't perfect.

Why This Book Exists

I didn't write this because I enjoy writing. I wrote it because I couldn't find a book that understood the real part of leadership, the quiet part. The part that lives between escalations and all-hands meetings, in WhatsApp messages at odd hours, in the little decisions that build trust or break it.

There are plenty of references for best practices. But very few that document best *practicals*. Most books talk about what leadership *should* look like. This one is about what it actually *feels* like, especially when things are messy, unfinished, uncertain.

I've been in rooms where the slides said one thing, but the hallway said something else entirely. I've had to defend decisions I didn't make, fix things I didn't break, and explain timelines I didn't own, because someone had to. And I've learned that leadership isn't about being the smartest in the room. It's about being the one who shows up when it counts.

Who This Book Is For

This is a book for people who lead by doing. For those who don't just give directions, they build momentum. For leaders who operate from inside the system, not above it. You might be a VP pulled into execution mode every day. A team lead trying to deliver without losing your people. A founder or program head carrying everything that slips through the cracks.

Whether or not your title says "Operations," if your calendar says firefight, patch, deliver, recover, this book is yours.

I've worn the operator's hat. But this isn't about job titles. It's about a kind of leadership that's rarely written about, the kind that isn't flashy, but foundational.

What This Book Is (and Isn't)

This isn't a playbook. It's not a list of hacks or models with neat acronyms. You won't find glossy frameworks or theoretical templates here. What you'll find are moments. Moments when I had to make decisions without full clarity. Moments I shielded my team from politics while pushing them to deliver. Moments I had to choose between what was easy, and what was necessary.

This book is leadership viewed through the lens of delivery. It's not meant to inspire with grandeur. It's meant to ground you in the real, operational and human.

How to Read This Book

Each chapter is a different lens. Some draw from tough calls I've had to make. Some are built around metaphors I've captured through photography. Some are lessons I didn't even realize were lessons until much later.

You can read it in order, or not. You can underline, dog-ear, or skip ahead. But if even one chapter gives you clarity when everything else feels murky, then this book has done its job.

Why Me? Why Now?

I'm not writing this as someone who has all the answers. I'm writing this as someone who's still in the arena.

Some of what's inside comes from decisions I'm proud of. Some comes from mistakes I wouldn't wish on anyone. But every piece of it is real.

Leadership isn't built in titles. It's built in small, quiet moments. It's built in the hours after everyone logs off, in the tone you choose under pressure, in the way you hold the line when no one is watching.

This book is for the people doing that work. If that's you, then this is yours.

Chapter 1: The Weight of a Leader's Words

"Clarity doesn't always arrive loudly. Sometimes, it breaks through like light in the fog."

It doesn't take a promotion to feel it. Sometimes, all it takes is one sentence, spoken too quickly, or too vaguely, and suddenly, everything around you begins to shift.

In leadership, your words carry more weight than you think. What you intend as a casual remark might be heard as a command. What you share as a half-formed thought might be received as a strategic direction. That's the strange burden of leadership, your intent doesn't always land the way you imagine.

I learned this the hard way. In one meeting, I offhandedly mentioned that we might need to consider restructuring our team to meet future demands. It wasn't a directive. It wasn't even a fully formed idea. But within a week, three team members had come to me privately to ask if they should start exploring other opportunities. One quietly updated his LinkedIn profile. In trying to think aloud, I had accidentally created a ripple of anxiety. That moment changed how I spoke as a leader.

Leadership Isn't Just Seen. It's Heard.

We often talk about presence in leadership, how we enter rooms, how we carry ourselves. But less often do we speak about tone, framing, and clarity. Yet what we say, and how we say it, often carries more weight than we realize.

Most misalignment in teams doesn't stem from a lack of communication. It comes from a surplus of casual communication. A leader's words aren't just processed; they're interpreted, rephrased, and often acted upon. You may never have explicitly said something, but your team might still act on what they *heard* you imply.

I've seen it countless times. A leader wonders, "Why did they do that? I never asked for it." But the more relevant question is: "What did they think I meant?"

Case Study: Satya Nadella and Clarity as Culture

When Satya Nadella took over Microsoft, he didn't begin with sweeping structural reforms. He began with language. He introduced words like *empathy*, *learning*, and *growth mindset* into daily vocabulary, words that felt almost out of place in a corporate environment known for its competitiveness.

But over time, these words became signals. And signals shaped culture. Employees started collaborating differently, taking ownership more freely, becoming more experimental in their thinking. What Nadella did was more than symbolic, it was structural. He used language as a lever for transformation.

Leadership doesn't just flow through org charts. It flows through the words we choose, repeat, and reinforce.

Your Casual Comments Are Often Taken Literally

This doesn't mean we need to walk on eggshells. It simply means that the higher you go, the louder your whispers become.

Small suggestions can spiral into action plans. Offhand remarks can morph into new processes. One stray sentence can set an entire team off course.

Over time, I began to use intentional phrases like, "This is just a thought experiment," or "Let's explore this, not execute it yet." These aren't disclaimers, they're precision tools. They protect clarity. They help the team discern between brainstorming and briefing.

In a world where attention is fragmented and interpretation is instant, clarity isn't optional. It's operational hygiene.

TOOL: The 5-Second Voice Audit

Before you end any meeting, take five seconds to pause and mentally check:

1. What did I *actually* say? Can I repeat it back verbatim?
2. How might it be interpreted by someone who is anxious, new, or eager to prove themselves?
3. Did I say anything vague that could create confusion or rework?
4. Did I leave the meeting with clarity or speculation?
5. Should I follow up in writing to clarify or confirm?

A better sentence today saves a hundred course corrections tomorrow.

War Leader Spotlight: Winston Churchill

Churchill wasn't always the most diplomatic leader. But he understood something many don't, people don't rally behind policies, they rally behind words that create belief.

During Britain's darkest hours, it wasn't military might that lifted the country, it was Churchill's language. "We shall fight on the beaches…" wasn't a tactical order. It was a psychological anchor. It gave people resolve.

In times of fear and fatigue, people follow clarity. And clarity often comes from the right sentence, spoken at the right time.

You don't have to be a great orator to be a leader. But you do need to master emotional clarity, especially when the stakes are high.

THINGS TO TRY

- **Voice Audit Practice:** After your next team call, write down exactly what you said, not what you *meant* to say. Compare this with how the team acted. Any gaps?
- **Clarity Checks:** Randomly ask one person after a meeting: "What's your understanding of what we're doing next?" Then compare it with your intention.

- **Language Inventory:** Over the next week, note the 3–5 phrases you use repeatedly. What do they signal, urgency, confidence, hesitation, doubt?

- **End With Alignment:** Before you log off or walk out, recap: What's been decided? What's still in exploration? Who's doing what? Speak it clearly. Write it down if needed.

Chapter 2 Leadership Is a Game of Perception, But Are You Seeing Clearly?

"Not everything we see is clear. And not everything unclear is untrue."

Perception shapes the path, long before reality catches up

Leadership isn't what you say it is. It's what others see it as.

You may think you're being transparent, your team thinks you're hiding something. You believe you're being decisive, they think you're being impulsive. You believe you're being empathetic, they think you're being vague.

Welcome to one of the hardest truths in leadership: perception is not reality, but it shapes how reality is received. The higher up you go, the more people interpret, not just your words, but your silences. They read into your tone, your pauses, your phrasing, even your calendar. And if you're not intentional about managing that perception, it will manage you.

This isn't about being performative. It's about being aware that your influence travels not only through decisions, but also through the signals you send, intentionally or not.

When Silence Speaks Louder Than Words

In my first year in a senior leadership role, I walked out of a high-stakes meeting and said nothing to my team. I was trying to gather my thoughts. But in that silence, people built stories.

"He looked worried." "Maybe the project is going off-track." "I think something big is coming."

None of that was true. But none of that was said by me either.

That moment taught me a valuable lesson: when you don't fill the gap with clarity, others will fill it with assumptions. And it's often the wrong ones.

War Leader Spotlight: Nelson Mandela

When Nelson Mandela took over post-apartheid South Africa, he faced an almost impossible leadership challenge, uniting a country that had been fractured for decades. The world watched every gesture, every handshake, every sentence.

He didn't get defensive. He got intentional.

He wore the Springboks jersey, a symbol once associated with the apartheid regime, during the 1995 Rugby World Cup. It wasn't just about sports. It was about shaping perception. About saying: *"This is all of ours now."*

Mandela didn't just lead policies. He led narratives. He understood that symbols can bridge trust faster than speeches.

What Does This Mean for Operators?

As operators, we often work in the background. We're building systems, fixing leaks, streamlining chaos. We pride ourselves on substance over noise. But let's be clear, substance without perception is often invisible.

If your efforts are not seen, they're not valued. If your leadership is misunderstood, it's not followed. If your decisions are not explained, they're questioned, or worse, resisted.

Operator's Tool: The Perception Filter Grid

Action or Behaviour	How You See It	How They Might See It
You stay quiet in meetings	Letting others lead	Disengaged or disinterested
You skip updates	Focused on execution	Hiding something or unprepared
You write curt emails	Time-saving brevity	Cold or annoyed
You change direction quickly	Agility	Confusion or lack of clarity

Use this grid to map the gap between *your intent* and *others' interpretation*. It's a deceptively simple tool, but once filled in, it can be a mirror and a map.

Instructions:

1. Print this out.
2. Add your own behaviors and how you believe they're perceived.
3. Share it with a trusted peer or team member.
4. Ask them to fill out *their* version.
5. Compare. Reflect. Realign.

You may not always be able to control how people see you, but you can take ownership of the signals you send. That's the *burden*, and the *power*, of leadership.

Things to Try

- **Pre-frame Important Decisions:** Before a big call or announcement, explain *why* a decision is being taken, not just *what* it is. Set the narrative, don't let others invent one.
- **Intent Clarity:** Replace vague affirmations like "Good job" with specific feedback. For example, "Your handling of the call yesterday showed great poise under pressure."
- **The Perception Audit:** For one week, ask yourself: "What do I want people to say about my leadership?" Then observe if your actions reflect that.
- **Feedback Loops:** Regularly ask one team member: *"What was your takeaway from that meeting?"* The gap between what you thought you communicated and what was heard is where perception gaps live.

Chapter 3 Great Leadership Is Built in Moments No One Sees

"Leadership isn't always a loud declaration. Sometimes, it's just one boat, holding its line in a fading light."

It happens when things break. When the strategy doesn't pan out. When the team is burnt out and timelines are wrecked. When you're staring at a whiteboard filled with crossed-out dependencies and broken promises, and no one to escalate to.

These are the moments that don't get posted on LinkedIn. No press release. No applause. Just you, and the quiet weight of decisions no one will ever see.

Leadership at the operational front isn't about bold declarations. It's about stabilizing before inspiring. Protecting momentum even when morale is fraying. Showing up, even when you don't have all the answers. The job isn't always to lift the team with vision, it's to keep things from falling apart long enough for clarity to return.

That's not weakness. That's the job.

In most organisations, recognition goes to the ones who present. Praise flows to those who launch. But every launch rests on invisible scaffolding, built, reinforced, and often rebuilt by people like you. This chapter is about them. About you. The people who lead in the quiet, unsung spaces that keep the machine running.

Let me offer a metaphor here.

If leadership were a corn cob, most people celebrate the shiny golden kernels on the outside. The visible wins. The talking points. But remove the spine inside, the hard, central core holding it all together, and the entire thing collapses. That's what you are in operations. You're not always visible. But you are what makes the system coherent. Whole. Functional.

It's not glamorous. But it's real.

Let's rewind to 1914. The ship *Endurance* is crushed by Antarctic ice, and Ernest Shackleton is stranded with 27 men. No backup plan. No rescue team. No comms. Just -40 degrees and a test of human resolve.

Most people only remember that everyone survived. What they forget is how. Shackleton didn't command with fire or flourish. He managed discipline, rotated routines to stave off mental breakdown, and kept communication tight and deliberate. In that crisis, there was no margin for performative leadership. He didn't need to motivate. He needed to stabilize.

And he did.

He treated emotional stability as a critical resource. The ability to hold belief together, not through speeches but through structure, presence, and calm, is what brought his crew home alive.

In operations, this lesson couldn't be more relevant. Teams don't fall apart all at once. They dissolve at the edges, through fatigue, indecision, and the slow erosion of confidence. It's the leader who steadies the rhythm, plugs invisible leaks, and quietly absorbs the tremors that prevents collapse.

So here's the reflection. What fires have you put out that no one saw? What decisions did you make that no one clapped for, but were essential for things to move? What friction did you absorb so your team could keep momentum?

That's real leadership. You don't need the room to know. You just need the room to keep working.

Let's make this practical.

I call this the "3AM Audit." Do it monthly.

Ask yourself:

1. What system would fall apart if I took my hands off it for a week?
2. Who on my team is quietly drowning while trying to hold everything together?
3. What have I fixed recently that no one knows about, but everything would have stalled without?

Your value doesn't always lie in the big calls. Sometimes, it's in being the one who doesn't let the small things fall apart.

To close, here are two small practices you can embed into your workflow:

1. The Invisible Wins Board Every week, capture moments of quiet execution, tech debts resolved, fires prevented, morale protected. Make it visible. Even if just for your own clarity.

2. The Stability Retrospective Each quarter, reflect on one moment where your presence made a difference. Not your strategy. Not your charm. Just you being there when it mattered.

This is where real culture is built. Not in town halls, but in tension. Not in alignment decks, but in the pauses between crisis and calm.

Shackleton didn't get a standing ovation. But he brought his people home.

You don't need to be celebrated. You just need to be steady.

Chapter 4: When Leadership Means Just Holding the Line

"Leadership doesn't always start with followers. Sometimes, you walk the bridge alone, until the world is ready to cross it with you."

It happens when things break.

When the strategy doesn't go according to plan.

When your team is burnt out, timelines are wrecked, and the escalation tree offers no answers.

You're staring at a whiteboard filled with dependencies, half-finished updates, and that one question you're not quite ready to say out loud: "What now?"

These are the moments that don't make it to LinkedIn. No press release. No applause. Just you, and the weight of decisions no one sees.

Leadership, especially at the operational front, rarely comes with fanfare. It doesn't always look like vision decks or charismatic town halls. More often, it looks like stabilizing before inspiring. It looks like holding momentum when morale is threadbare, showing up again and again even when you're running on fumes, and deciding what must be protected when everything else is falling apart.

Sometimes, you're not building. You're not transforming. You're not innovating. You're just holding things together, with duct tape, doubt, and sheer will.

And that's still leadership.

Because when the engine stutters, someone still has to steer.

It's easy to confuse movement with progress. Urgency gives the illusion of action. But if you're not careful, what looks like speed might just be the wobble you've been ignoring for far too long.

In these moments, the most important leadership act isn't to charge ahead, it's to anchor. Operational leadership isn't always about driving bold decisions. Sometimes, it's about absorbing the shocks. Protecting the pace. Buying your team just enough time to catch their breath and carry forward.

I've seen it. Teams moving on the surface while unspoken tensions churn underneath. The metrics look green, but the energy in the room is brittle. No one wants to say it, but something is off.

I call this the corncob moment.

From a distance, it looks full. But up close, there are gaps, missing kernels, dropped balls, silent hesitations. That's your early signal. Ignore it, and you'll find yourself patching up a mess that could have been prevented. Listen to it, and you might just hold the system steady long enough to reset.

This is where leadership becomes less about strategy and more about structure.

You don't just set direction. You create emotional buffers. You become the human version of a shock absorber, managing conflict, holding trust, and choosing to stay grounded when everyone else is bracing for impact.

History has shown us what this looks like. In 1914, Ernest Shackleton and his crew were stranded on the Antarctic ice after their ship, *Endurance*, was crushed. No help. No plan. Just twenty-seven men and brutal conditions.

Shackleton didn't resort to big speeches or delusions of grandeur. He stabilized. He rotated tasks. He enforced daily routines. He made sure every small thing, from mealtimes to movement, created structure and focus. He kept the team engaged, present, and psychologically afloat.

Not a single life was lost.

That's crisis leadership. Not as it's romanticized, but as it's lived, messy, human, and full of quiet resolve.

It's what separates the leaders who weather storms from those who contribute to the chaos.

So here's the truth: not every leader needs to disrupt. Some of us are here to endure. To hold the line long enough for the next move to become possible.

Because sometimes, the most powerful form of leadership is simply not letting the damn thing fall apart.

Toolkit: The 3-R Stability Framework

When the plan breaks and the pressure builds, pause and run this simple loop:

1. **Rhythm** – Are we maintaining healthy team rituals, not just output?
2. **Reinforcement** – Are we reinforcing clarity at every friction point?
3. **Resilience** – Are we spotting burnout early and responding fast?

This isn't about slowing down. It's about ensuring your team doesn't break while trying to move too fast.

Things to Try This Week

- Pick a day this week and pause all new initiatives. Just listen.
- Do a "green-check" huddle: ask your team if everything that looks fine on the dashboard *feels* fine.

- Close one loop that's been silently hanging. It will restore more momentum than you think.
- Create one 20-minute buffer each day just to check in, with yourself, and with your team, not on progress, but on pressure.

Chapter 5: The Kindest Leaders Still Carry the Heaviest Light

"The kindest leaders rarely shine the brightest. But they're the ones who carry the light the furthest."

Empathy is often misunderstood in leadership. It's mistaken for indulgence, seen as softness, or dismissed as a liability in high-performance environments. But the truth is more complicated. The most compassionate leaders often shoulder the hardest truths. They carry not just the responsibility to perform but the emotional load of the people who rely on them.

There's a tension here that rarely gets named. The more attuned you are to people's needs, the more they bring those needs to you. Their stress, confusion, fear, and burnout show up at your door, not because you're the cause, but because you're the safe space. And so you listen. You support. You show patience when it's easier to escalate. You make room for off days and still find a way to meet deadlines. But beneath it all, you carry the weight, quietly, constantly, and often without acknowledgment.

Over time, this kind of leadership can become invisible. Your steadiness is expected. Your calm is taken for granted. And the kindness you extend becomes part of the operating system, not something worth noticing. But that doesn't make it less vital. In fact, it's what keeps the engine from overheating.

The challenge is in the balance. Because empathy without boundaries is unsustainable. And authority without care is unsuited to today's workplace. Leaders today need to manage both. They must be trusted without being overrun, decisive without being distant, and emotionally available without becoming emotionally depleted.

I faced this paradox a few years ago during a critical retention cycle. Our numbers were down, team energy was dropping, and the usual push tactics weren't working. People were showing up, but their momentum was missing. It wasn't just a performance issue, it was emotional exhaustion.

And as the leader, I had two choices: crack down harder, or ease up and risk further dip.

Instead, I did something else entirely. I paused everything and got the team into a room, not for a performance review, but for a conversation. We acknowledged what wasn't working, laid down what was expected, and created space to discuss what we needed to do differently. The targets didn't change. But how we reached them did. We cut out non-essential tasks. We introduced half-day sprints with recovery time. We redistributed pressure in a way that didn't compromise outcomes but allowed people to catch their breath. Some misused the grace; most didn't. Because when people feel genuinely seen and supported, they often self-correct.

We didn't lose momentum. We gained trust. And that trust became the foundation for the performance turnaround that followed.

This kind of leadership, human-centered but outcome-aware, is not about being liked. It's about being dependable. It's about holding your team's weight without letting go of the mission. And sometimes, it means carrying setbacks alone so that others can stay focused on progress.

Arvind Krishna's tenure as CEO of IBM is a case study in this kind of leadership. When he stepped into the role in 2020, he inherited a legacy institution wrestling with structural fatigue, declining relevance, and a global crisis that had changed how people worked and what they expected from their workplaces. His response wasn't driven by theatrics or overselling a turnaround story. It was measured, decisive, and deeply human.

He led IBM through a series of significant shifts, most notably the spin-off of its legacy infrastructure services, while simultaneously repositioning the company around hybrid cloud and AI. These weren't easy decisions. They meant breaking from the familiar, taking on investor skepticism, and asking employees to stretch into unfamiliar roles. But Krishna didn't hide the difficulty. He addressed it. He explained not just what was changing but why it mattered. He advocated for hybrid work but didn't glorify it. He was candid about layoffs but equally focused on reinvention. Through it all, he demonstrated that clarity and empathy are not mutually exclusive. One strengthens the other when delivered with integrity.

Leaders like Krishna show that authority doesn't have to be loud to be firm. And empathy, when embedded into decisions and structures, not just conversations, can scale across large, complex organizations.

For many leaders operating in the middle of chaos, the question isn't whether to be kind or commanding. The real challenge is knowing how to sequence both. It's in learning when to make room and when to make calls. When to listen without fixing, and when to act without delay. This dance isn't formulaic. It's contextual. It requires emotional fluency and situational judgment. It requires the leader to be more than just a function. It requires them to be human, but grounded.

Tools & Frameworks

To lead with both empathy and authority, it helps to visualize where your current style sits. One useful mental model is what I call the **Empathy–Authority Grid**. On one axis is empathy, ranging from low to high. On the other, authority. When both are low, you're a bystander, present but ineffective. When empathy is low and authority is high, you risk becoming a control-oriented enforcer, one who achieves compliance but not commitment. When empathy is high and authority low, you drift into the burnout zone, overfunctioning on behalf of your team, absorbing more than is sustainable. The ideal zone is where both empathy and authority are high. That's the zone of the Empowerer: the leader who creates clarity without coldness and provides care without coddling.

Another tool I've found helpful in difficult moments is the **Setback Shield**. It's not a mechanism for hiding failure but a lens for processing it before broadcasting it. When something goes wrong, and in operations, something always will, I ask myself three questions before bringing it to the team. First: Does this need to be shared now, or can it wait until I've processed it better? Second: What's the learning here, and how do I make it useful without letting it demoralize? And third: Am I sharing this to solve something, or to offload emotional residue I haven't worked through? This shield doesn't block truth; it paces it. It helps me lead through crisis with steadiness, not reaction.

Tips to Try

1. **Audit Your Interactions Weekly** Each week, reflect on whether you offered support without also reinforcing direction. Did you listen without leading? Or direct without understanding? Leadership is in the balance, track how often you calibrate.

2. **Narrate Decisions with 'Why'** When you make a tough call, don't just communicate the what. Explain the why. Context builds credibility, even when people don't agree with the outcome.

3. **Introduce Micro-Resets During Burnout Cycles** If your team is hitting emotional fatigue, try introducing 90-minute focused sprints followed by short, intentional pauses. This shows you value output, but not at the cost of wellbeing.

4. **Model Resilience, Not Suppression** When you face setbacks, share how you're navigating through, not just the fact that you're struggling. Demonstrate what healthy recovery looks like, especially when others are watching.

5. **Clarify Emotional Boundaries** Being approachable doesn't mean being available for everything. Let your team know when you can listen and help, and when you need time to process on your own. Boundaries are part of sustainability.

Empathy makes you trustworthy. Authority makes you effective. But only when held together, intentionally, consistently, and without apology, do they make you a leader worth following. And sometimes, the strongest leaders are the ones who speak last, listen hardest, and quietly carry the weight no one else sees.

Because the kindest leaders still carry the heaviest light. And they do it not for recognition, but because they know: someone has to.

Chapter 6: When Leadership Means Letting Go

There's a strange paradox in leadership. The further you rise, the more you're expected to hold. Yet the most mature decisions often involve releasing that hold, on control, on outcomes, on your own way of doing things. Letting go doesn't mean walking away. It means trusting that what you've built can stand, even without your constant grip.

Most leadership books celebrate decisiveness, presence, and execution. Far fewer talk about restraint. But operational leadership, especially in high-scale environments, teaches you something most manuals miss: that control is not the same as stability, and presence is not the same as involvement. The real test of leadership comes not when you're in the thick of action, but when you're deliberately choosing not to be.

Letting go doesn't always look dramatic. Sometimes it's a small moment: not responding to a message you would have usually stepped into, allowing someone else to present in a room where you were once the anchor, or choosing not to double-check what you would have reviewed line by line just months earlier. But make no mistake, these moments require courage. Because what you're letting go of is not just the task. It's your sense of control, your legacy in motion, and your fear of things breaking without you.

I remember the shift clearly. It was six months into a structural change we had pushed through across the academic operations of our partner universities. The transition had been hard-fought. Systems had to be redesigned. Calendars recalibrated. Faculty alignment brought under a single framework. I had been closely involved, every tracker, every escalation, every single piece of delivery had my fingerprints on it.

Then came the second semester under the new structure. This was the moment to let the system run. But I couldn't sit still. I kept asking for daily updates. I reviewed dashboards I didn't need to. I intervened in meeting threads meant for managers. Until one of my senior team members quietly pulled me aside and said, "It's working. But it won't if you don't let us lead."

That line landed hard. Not because it was wrong, but because it was right.

I had built the system to scale, but I was still operating like I was running a pilot. I was holding on, not out of distrust, but habit. What I didn't realize was that by refusing to step back, I was slowing the very autonomy I claimed to enable.

So I let go. Not all at once. But intentionally.

I stopped attending every review. I asked for only two updates a week. I created decision thresholds, guidelines that clarified when I needed to be looped in and when I didn't. Most importantly, I told the team I trusted their judgment. And then I showed it by not interfering.

What happened next was a reminder of why letting go is a power move, not a passive one.

The team rose. Decisions got faster. Ownership deepened. People stopped seeking permission for every deviation and started offering solutions. The structure I had once held together was now holding itself, and holding others.

This wasn't abdication. It was leadership, practiced through withdrawal. And that changed everything.

Tools & Frameworks

One of the mental models I now use often is something I call the *Involvement Threshold Framework*. It's a simple tool to help leaders assess when to step in, and when to step back. Picture three concentric circles:

- **Circle 1: Must Lead** – These are high-stakes, strategic, or reputationally sensitive matters. As a leader, your involvement is essential.
- **Circle 2: Must Shape** – These are operationally important but can be delegated. You shape the intent or set the bar, but execution lives elsewhere.
- **Circle 3: Must Let Go** – These are tasks or issues where your presence adds friction, not value. If others can handle it 80% as well, let them.

This framework helped me build internal clarity around my own impulses. Every time I felt the urge to jump in, I would ask: which circle does this fall in? More often than not, I found I was overreaching into the third circle, micromanaging under the guise of support.

Another useful mindset I adopted was the idea of *Ownership Signaling*. This is about visibly handing over responsibility in ways that communicate trust, not abandonment. For example, when I stepped back from leading cluster reviews, I publicly nominated the next point person, ensured they had access to all data and context, and announced to all stakeholders that they had my full backing. This wasn't just about efficiency, it was about creating psychological safety for them to lead.

Tips to Try

1. **Run a Weekly Grip Audit** At the end of each week, list five things you controlled that could have been delegated. Then list one thing you should have intervened in but didn't. The gap reveals your current instinct profile.

2. **Narrate the Exit, Not Just the Entry** Most leaders explain when they step into a role or project. But learning to narrate your withdrawal is just as powerful. Let your team know why you're stepping back, and how that's a sign of trust, not distance.

3. **Install Decision Gates, Not Permission Loops** Instead of reviewing every action, create clear decision gates, milestones or thresholds that trigger your involvement. This empowers teams while still giving you control where it counts.

4. **Celebrate Independent Wins Publicly** When a team delivers in your absence, celebrate not just the outcome but the fact that they did it without you. This reinforces that autonomy is not just allowed, it's recognized.

5. **Create Let-Go Rituals** Every quarter, choose one responsibility or review to let go of. Treat it like a promotion for the team, not a loss for yourself. Document the handoff, share the rationale, and let it go completely.

Letting go is not an act of indifference. It's an act of belief. It's a decision to trust your team, your systems, and the direction you've already set in motion. It's what allows you to move from being the operator to being the orchestrator. And it's what gives your people the room to grow beyond your shadow.

The strongest leaders aren't those who control everything. They're the ones who know exactly what to hold, and what to release.

"Sometimes the hardest move isn't stepping up. It's stepping back, so someone else can rise."

The dew drop never clings too long. It reflects the world around it, carries weight with grace, and when the moment comes, lets go. That's not surrender. That's timing. That's wisdom. And that's leadership.

Chapter 7: What You Carry, Alone

"No one sees the weight in your boat. They only watch it glide."

There's a part of leadership no one prepares you for. It's not the decision-making, the pressure, or even the constant drive for performance. Those, with time and experience, become familiar. The part that remains unspoken, the part that stays quietly heavy, is the burden you carry that no one else can.

This burden isn't visible. It doesn't show up in dashboards or debriefs. It isn't mentioned in onboarding or taught in leadership workshops. But it's there. It builds over time. And it changes you.

Because the more responsibility you hold, the more you start absorbing what others never see. You begin to carry the misjudgments you can't walk back, the errors you must correct silently, and the decisions that protect the team but cost you personally. You carry the tension of knowing the real story behind a failure, the one you'll never explain publicly, because doing so would only transfer pain downward. You carry the instinct to shield, quietly, efficiently, and without expecting applause.

As your role expands, the spotlight may widen, but the space for reflection contracts. You become the one who must remain steady when others are shaken. You hold the emotional temperature of the room. You modulate your responses not because you're unbothered, but because you understand the impact of losing composure. It's not performance. It's responsibility.

I've lived through these moments. One of the most instructive came during what should have been a simple operational shift, an internal change to optimize workflows across teams. I approved the plan. The logic was clear. The intent was solid. On paper, the efficiencies made sense. But two weeks in, it was obvious something was off. Delays crept in, and team friction grew. The system we had launched to simplify execution had inadvertently made some parts of the process worse.

Most people only saw symptoms, late updates, minor escalations, delays in coordination. But I saw the root cause, and I knew it traced back to a decision I had made. No one else had the full view. No one else needed to. It was my call. My responsibility.

So I absorbed it. I didn't redirect the blame. I didn't explain my rationale in long emails. I met the impacted teams, acknowledged the gaps, and stayed back late for the next two weeks helping patch what had come undone. Quietly. Without making it a teaching moment. Because this wasn't the time to teach. It was the time to own.

No one applauded. No one needed to. But that's what this kind of leadership looks like, holding things together without needing to be seen doing it.

This isn't about martyrdom. It's about maturity. The discipline to carry your doubts without burdening the team with them. The capacity to process failure without using your people as an outlet. And the clarity to know that not everything needs to be fixed publicly to be fixed well.

There is a loneliness here. One that even your closest colleagues can't always reach. It's not because they don't care, it's because this part of the journey isn't theirs to carry. It's yours. And over time, you learn to make peace with that.

But you also learn something else: that these moments build not just your resilience, but your depth. The setbacks you carry in silence often teach you more than the wins you celebrate aloud. They give you the insight to build better systems. The empathy to coach without condescension. And the grounding to lead without theatrics.

Eventually, you stop seeing this burden as a flaw of the role. You start seeing it as a quiet privilege, the ability to take what's hard and make it easier for others. The strength to carry what's painful so others can stay focused. The choice to remain composed not because it's easy, but because your steadiness might be what keeps the team from unraveling.

That's not weakness. That's leadership.

Tools & Frameworks

When I find myself in the middle of these moments, when something has gone wrong, and I know it sits on my shoulders, I turn to a simple internal tool: the *Leadership Pressure Compass*. It helps me manage what I'm feeling without offloading it onto the team. The process is reflective, not reactive. I ask myself three things:

First, is this pressure I'm feeling purely from this incident, or is it layered over something unresolved from the past? Second, does my team need to be shielded from this right now, or do they need to see some of the mess to grow from it? And third, if I speak now, will I create clarity, or will I just be transferring my own stress onto them?

These questions don't provide instant answers, but they create a buffer. That pause is often enough to stop a poor decision from being made under emotional pressure.

Another tool I've relied on over the years is the *Reflection Ledger*. It's not a journal. It's a private log where I record leadership moments that didn't go well. I document what happened, how I responded, and what I wish I had done differently. It's simple, factual, and emotion-neutral. I don't write to vent, I write to remember. That ledger is my private curriculum. And reviewing it every few months reminds me of how often I've course-corrected without fanfare.

Tips to Try

1. **Designate a Weekly Reflection Window** Create ten minutes of uninterrupted space every week to reflect on what you carried that

week but didn't share. No agenda, just space to acknowledge your own effort.

2. **Practice Discreet Ownership** When you make a decision that doesn't land well, don't explain it immediately unless required. Take ownership first, fix the impact, and explain only if it adds value, not validation.

3. **Build a Setback SOP** Develop your own protocol for handling internal failure. Mine is simple: pause $\rightarrow$ assess $\rightarrow$ act $\rightarrow$ communicate $\rightarrow$ debrief. It removes panic from the equation.

4. **Log, Don't Linger** When something goes wrong, write it down factually, what happened, what you learned, what you'll do next time. Then close the log and move on.

5. **Normalize Quiet Strength** At least once a quarter, share with someone trusted what you've handled silently. Not to seek sympathy, but to remind yourself that being strong doesn't mean staying isolated.

You will carry things as a leader that no one else sees. That's not a failure. That's not an imbalance. That's part of the role. And over time, you come to accept that some of the most important things you will do won't be celebrated. They won't even be noticed.

But they will be felt, by the people who got to do their best work because you were strong enough to carry the weight they never had to see.

That's the quiet grace of leadership. And it's often what defines the leader more than any metric ever will.

Chapter 8: The War Inside the Room

"Not every war erupts. Some just flicker, quiet, guarded, and glowing behind chains of decorum."

Not all battles are fought out loud.

Some unfold across spreadsheets, timelines, and meetings that run five minutes longer than they should. They're dressed in civility but charged with resistance. No one shouts. But no one concedes either.

These are the wars inside the room, the ones where ego, priorities, and pressure collide.

For operational leaders, this is the real battlefield. Not the field visit. Not the annual review. But the moment when what you know is right runs into what someone else is unwilling to change. The tension isn't always open. Sometimes it's polite. Sometimes it's passive. Sometimes it comes with a smile. But you feel it all the same.

It starts small. A plan you've built gets challenged. A process you've redesigned is sidelined. A meeting meant to finalize something turns into a debate you didn't ask for. And suddenly, you're no longer presenting, you're defending.

You know the data. You've done the groundwork. But in that moment, the room has shifted. The conversation isn't about logic anymore. It's about control.

I've been in these rooms more times than I care to count. Rooms where a breakthrough was on the table, but so was someone's legacy. Rooms where the right thing was clear, but saying it out loud might break a fragile alliance. Rooms where I had to decide: push forward and risk fracture, or pull back and live with a diluted outcome.

There's no playbook for these moments. Just instinct, restraint, and the ability to read the unspoken.

Early in my career, I thought these rooms were about winning arguments. I came in ready, with slides, with notes, with counterpoints. What I learned, after a few bruising experiences, is that winning the room often means changing your posture, not raising your volume. You can't outpower resistance. You have to outwait it, outwork it, or outlast it.

Sometimes, it means absorbing the hit and playing the long game.

Sometimes, it means letting the other side speak first, even when you know their version is incomplete, because what they need isn't correction, but dignity.

And sometimes, it means walking away with a partial win, because today's compromise buys tomorrow's breakthrough.

That doesn't make you weak. That makes you strategic.

Lessons from the War Leaders

When I think about leadership under pressure, I often return to **Abraham Lincoln**, a man surrounded by internal conflict even within his own cabinet. He wasn't just leading a nation through civil war; he was leading a team that didn't always believe in him. But Lincoln didn't react to every slight. He didn't demand loyalty at the cost of candor. He held space for disagreement, even as he held the Union together. In many ways, he won the war inside the room before he ever won it on the battlefield.

Then there's **Joan of Arc**, young, untrained, yet unshakable in conviction. She stood in front of men who dismissed her before she even spoke. Her presence in rooms she was never meant to enter was itself a form of leadership. She didn't wait for permission to believe what she saw. She made her case with clarity, and when needed, carried the consequence of being right too early.

Chanakya, the ancient strategist, played an entirely different game. He wasn't loud. He wasn't visible. But he knew how power worked, and how to bend systems without breaking them. When confronted with resistance, he didn't fight it head-on. He studied it, timed it, and then turned it to his advantage. His genius wasn't in force. It was in foresight.

And then there's **Ernest Shackleton**, a leader who didn't win with vision decks, but with presence. Trapped in ice, thousands of miles from civilization, he held his crew together for over a year without a single loss of life. Not because he had all the answers, but because he knew when to hold the line and when to let others breathe. He led through trust, not tyranny.

These leaders operated in radically different worlds. But they all understood one thing: the most consequential leadership happens when no one is cheering, when tension is high, and when you must choose between pride and progress.

Tools & Frameworks

One framework I've found useful in high-friction rooms is what I call the **Conflict Posture Map**. It helps me decide how to respond based not just on what's right, but on what the moment requires.

There are four postures:

1. **Anchor** – Hold your position calmly, even when others push. Use this when the principle at stake is non-negotiable.
2. **Mirror** – Reflect what others are saying to build trust before you introduce your view. Use this when you're trying to lower defenses.
3. **Shift** – Change the frame of the conversation. If you can't win on detail, shift to intent. If you can't agree on method, align on outcome.
4. **Exit** – Step away strategically. Not every war is won in one meeting. Sometimes, leaving the table protects your position better than staying in it.

I also use a **Fracture Forecast** before high-stakes meetings. It's a 3-point preparation lens:

- **What am I willing to compromise on?**
- **What is non-negotiable?**
- **What's the emotional temperature of the room, and who controls it?**

Knowing this doesn't make conflict go away. But it prevents me from getting blindsided.

Tips to Try

1. **Never Enter a Room Needing to Win** The minute your self-worth is tied to being right, you've already lost leverage. Enter to influence, not to impress.

2. **Separate Friction from Disrespect** Pushback is not personal. Don't escalate every disagreement into a stand. Learn to distinguish posture from principle.

3. **Use Strategic Silence** In moments of tension, don't rush to fill the silence. Let others wrestle with what you've said. Silence can be the loudest statement in the room.

4. **Rehearse Your Flex Points** Before high-stakes meetings, rehearse not just your message, but your concessions. Know what you can yield on, and how to frame it as alignment, not retreat.

5. **Win the Long Game, Not the Moment** Don't trade future buy-in for short-term control. Let people keep face today, if it means they'll trust your leadership tomorrow.

Leadership doesn't always look like standing at the front. Sometimes, it looks like sitting at the edge of the room, watching a conversation unfold, and knowing exactly when to speak and when to wait.

You'll fight many wars inside the room. Not all of them are worth winning. But the ones that are, will test your patience, your posture, and your principles.

And how you show up in those moments will define far more than your ideas. It will define your legacy.

Chapter **9**: The Cost of Clarity

"Clarity sharpens your view, but it can also distance you from the familiar. That's the cost of seeing things as they are."

Clarity is easy to admire from a distance. It looks like decisiveness. It feels like strength. But up close, it rarely feels that simple. Because real clarity comes with consequence.

People say they want clear plans, defined roles, transparent expectations. But what they often mean is: "Give me clarity, until it affects what I'm used to." In practice, clarity disrupts. It calls out inefficiency. It eliminates grey zones. It makes visible what many preferred to keep hidden.

For operators, this is the turning point. Clarity isn't just a virtue. It's a risk. Because the moment you start drawing lines, on roles, timelines, or scope, you begin to threaten the unwritten rules people have grown comfortable with.

When I took over operations across our academic systems, the most visible issue wasn't performance, it was overload. Our course catalogue was sprawling: over 550 subjects offered across various programs. On the surface, it seemed like abundance. But when we examined what sat underneath, we found confusion, duplication, and logistical strain.

Faculty were overextended, students were scattered across redundant electives, and the systems team was constantly patching things that should never have been approved in the first place. Content wasn't consistently updated. Feedback loops were broken. And there was no unified structure for delivery.

We could have kept pushing the same cycle forward. But clarity demanded something else.

So we stripped it all down. We built a tracker from the ground up. We mapped every course to its content readiness, student load, and operational bandwidth. We benchmarked each subject for relevance, recurrence, and readiness. If a course didn't meet those criteria, it was paused. Some were dropped.

In less than one semester, we reduced the catalogue from over 550 courses to 192.

It was the right call. But it came at a cost.

Stakeholders who had built their comfort around certain course structures pushed back. Faculty saw the move as limiting. Some teams felt threatened, interpreting the reduction as loss rather than focus. There were questions, criticisms, even suggestions that we were "oversimplifying" an academic ecosystem that had taken years to build.

But that ecosystem had grown by addition, not intention. And what it needed was not preservation, but clarity.

What I didn't expect, though, was how personally some of the resistance would land. Even when it wasn't directed at me, it felt directed through me. Because I had drawn the line. Because I had said "this won't work" when it would have been easier to say nothing.

That's the hidden tax of clarity. You may be solving for the system, but you still have to carry the weight of how people feel about it.

It would have been tempting to backtrack, to soften the structure, to delay the implementation, to let a few exceptions in. But we held the line. Not because we were stubborn, but because we were sure. We had the data. We had the patterns. And we knew that holding this moment would help everything else move faster later.

And it did.

In the months that followed, delivery cycles improved. Academic planning stabilized. Escalations dropped. Faculty prep time increased. Learner communication became timely. And more importantly, the system became predictable. That predictability created trust, not just in the system, but in us.

No one clapped when it happened. But they noticed when things worked.

That's the job. And that's the cost of clarity.

Tools & Frameworks

One of the tools that helped guide this decision-making was something I call the **R³ Lens**, a simple but rigorous filter I apply to any system we're trying to clean up: *Relevance, Recurrence*, and *Readiness*. Each proposed element, whether it's a course, a campaign, or a workflow, must pass through these three questions:

- Is it relevant to our goals or learner needs right now?
- Is it something we can run repeatedly, not just once?
- Is the team and infrastructure ready to deliver it at scale?

If it fails on two or more, it doesn't make the cut. This isn't about over-indexing on efficiency. It's about ensuring that everything we offer has a reason, a rhythm, and a runway.

Another framework I lean on is the **Clarity Shock Cycle**. I've seen the same arc repeat itself each time we introduce structure into a previously ambiguous space:

1. **Discomfort** – People are rattled by the change.
2. **Pushback** – Resistance peaks, often from those most impacted.
3. **Adjustment** – Teams start to work within the new rules, hesitantly.
4. **Adoption** – New habits take root.
5. **Attribution** – Eventually, people forget it was even a change, and clarity becomes the new norm.

Knowing this arc helps me stay steady when feedback gets noisy. It reminds me that early resistance is not a sign of failure, it's just the price of focus.

Tips to Try

1. **Define Clarity Before You Deliver It** Before rolling out a new structure or decision, define what clarity looks like for each stakeholder group. Clarity for one team may feel like constraint to another.
2. **Use Visual Frameworks** Don't just say the system is changing, show it. Diagrams, filters, checklists, these reduce ambiguity and help people process disruption.
3. **Hold Through the Dip** Expect the middle phase, right after change, before results, to feel unappreciated. Your job is to hold through that dip.
4. **Let the System Speak First** When questioned, let early wins and emerging stability do the talking. Don't defend everything verbally. Let performance tell the story.
5. **Document What Was Broken** Archive the confusion the new structure replaced. One day, when people ask why you changed things, you'll have the receipts.

Clarity is not always popular. It rarely feels heroic. But it builds systems that last.

It removes luck from success. It replaces reactivity with rhythm. And it gives your team something precious: the ability to plan, not just cope.

It won't always be appreciated immediately. But if you do it right, your impact will outlast your presence.

And that's the kind of legacy every operator should aim for.

Chapter **10**: Built to Be Invisible

"You weren't seen. But everything stood because of you."

There's a certain kind of leadership that doesn't announce itself.

It doesn't begin meetings with declarations. It doesn't carry titles like "visionary" or "changemaker." It doesn't need to be the loudest in the room.

Instead, it shows up early. It studies systems. It closes gaps. It moves pieces into place until the entire machine begins to run with a hum so smooth that no one remembers how broken things once were.

That's operational leadership. And it's built to be invisible.

Most people don't notice the water until it stops flowing. They don't notice the structure until it fails. The operator's job is to ensure they never have to.

If leadership is often measured by visibility, then operators have always played a different game. Our victories are quiet. Our impact is cumulative. And our reward, more often than not, is the absence of chaos.

The truth is, when you're doing your job well as an operator, no one talks about it. The systems work. The plans hold. The escalations drop. The energy stabilizes. People assume that's how it was always supposed to be.

But you know better.

You remember what it took to get there, the messy whiteboards, the rewired schedules, the late-night fixes, the hard conversations that didn't go on record. You remember the days when the only thing holding the structure together was your belief that it could get better.

And you kept going.

Not because someone promised recognition. But because you understood what was at stake if you didn't.

This work, this mindset, isn't for everyone. It requires a strange blend of humility and control. You have to want the system to win more than you want the credit. You have to be okay with your best work being absorbed into the routine. You have to find satisfaction not in applause, but in stability.

There's something beautiful about that.

Because while others chase attention, you chase alignment. While others seek to be known, you work to make things known, clear, consistent, dependable.

You build systems that outlast you. You create patterns that don't need you. You don't insert yourself into every process, you design yourself out of them, so others can step in.

And in doing so, you create something far rarer than influence.

You create trust.

Tools & Frameworks

At this point in the journey, the tools are no longer just frameworks. They are reflexes. But there's one I've always carried with me, the **Invisibility Index**.

It's a self-check, done quarterly, where I ask:

1. What systems now work without me?
2. What team decisions no longer need my approval?
3. What friction has silently disappeared in the last three months?
4. Who has grown into my old space, and how have I made room for that?

This isn't about stepping away. It's about stepping back just enough to test whether the structure holds.

Because the real goal of an operator isn't to be indispensable. It's to make the system so strong that you no longer have to rescue it.

Tips to Try

1. **Design for Transfer, Not Tenure** Build systems that others can inherit. Document your logic. Leave behind a map, not a mystery.
2. **Let Reliability Be the Reward** Not every win needs a headline. Quiet weeks are often your greatest proof of impact.
3. **Audit Your Own Shadow** Every six months, look at where your presence is still required and ask: is this because the task is critical, or because I haven't yet built enough trust or process?
4. **Protect the System, Not Your Role** The more you tie value to your visibility, the harder it becomes to scale. Focus on the system's success, even if it outgrows you.
5. **Exit Clean, Not Loud** When you hand something off, don't linger. Make the transition seamless, and then move forward. Your best legacy will be how little they needed you after you left.

This isn't about silence. It's about substance. The kind that doesn't need to be amplified to be real. Operational leadership isn't measured by how loudly it echoes, but by how deeply it holds. By the strength of the systems left behind. By the way people continue to move forward, even when you're no longer in the room.

The best operators don't just fix what's broken. They reshape what's possible. They don't chase permanence or visibility. They focus on building patterns that others can repeat, structures that can scale, and environments that run smoothly long after their names fade from the workflow.

When they move on, they don't leave behind applause. They leave behind momentum.

You may never be the face of transformation. But you were the reason it held together. You weren't the story. But the story moved because of you.

And while others are still watching what you built, you've already moved on, working at the next layer, solving the next problem, building the next system that no one sees coming.

Because this was never meant to be the whole playbook. It was just the foundation.

Epilogue

If you've made it this far, you're not just reading. You're leading. You're building. You've felt the weight of things no one else sees, and you've stayed in the work anyway.

This book wasn't written to teach you how to operate. If these chapters resonated, chances are you already do. It was written to remind you that your kind of leadership, the kind that stabilizes, aligns, fixes, and quietly scales, is not a footnote in the leadership canon. It's the spine.

There are no standing ovations for systems that work flawlessly. No applause for meetings that end early because everything was thought through in advance. No headlines for the operator who de-escalated the crisis before it even began. But in that silence lies something powerful: trust. Dependability. And legacy.

Your work will not always be seen. That's not the point. What matters is that it holds.

So take what you found in these pages and do what you do best, adapt it. Apply it. Push back on it. Leave behind what doesn't serve your context. But don't stop building. Don't stop showing up with clarity, with intent, with the quiet confidence that comes from knowing how things are really held together.

Because this was never the full playbook. It was only the foundation. And when the next layer is ready, you'll be ready too.